Contents

Awesome junk

Don't throw away your junk! Turn it into fabulous pieces of art instead. Did you know that you can make puppets, robots, fairy-tale castles and hanging monkey door frames from junk? In this book we'll show you how!

Find out how awesome junk art can be.

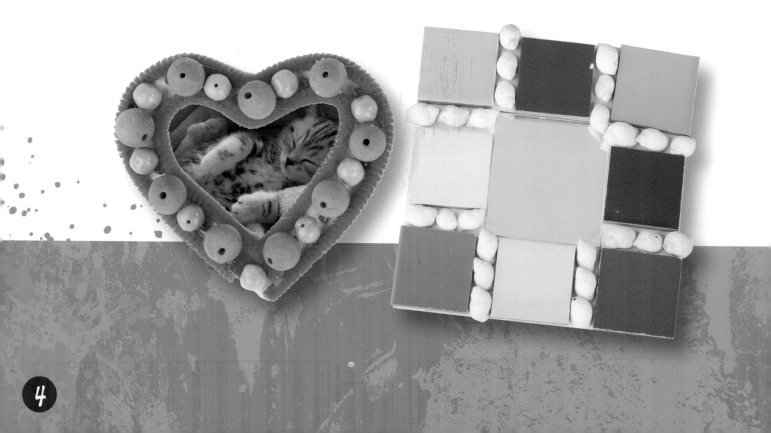

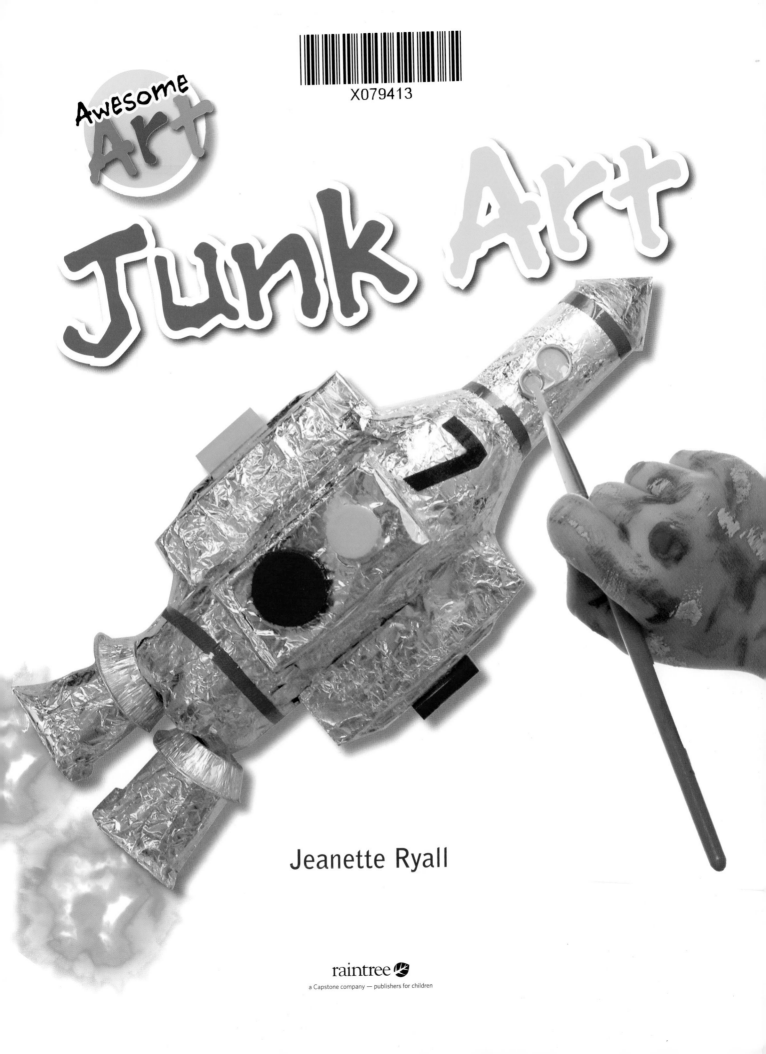

Junk Art

Awesome Art

Jeanette Ryall

raintree
a Capstone company — publishers for children

Raintree is an imprint of Capstone Global Library Limited, a company incorporated in England and Wales having its registered office at 264 Banbury Road, Oxford, OX2 7DY – Registered company number: 6695582

www.raintree.co.uk
myorders@raintree.co.uk

Produced for Raintree by Calcium
Edited by Sara Antill
Designed by Jeanette Ryall
Original illustrations © Capstone Global Library Limited 2020
Originated by Capstone Global Library Ltd
Printed and bound in India

978 1 3982 0031 9 (hardback)
978 1 3982 0035 7 (paperback)

British Library Cataloguing in Publication Data
A full catalogue record for this book is available from the British Library.

Acknowledgements
We would like to thank the following for permission to reproduce photographs: Cover: Jeanette Ryall l, Shutterstock P J Cross r. Inside: pp. 4–5: Tudor Photography; pp. 6–7: (main) Tudor Photography, (steps) Tudor Photography; pp. 8: (main) Jeanette Ryall; pp. 8–9: (steps) Tudor Photography; p. 9: (main) Tudor Photography; pp. 10–11: (steps) Tudor Photography; p. 11: (main) Tudor Photography; pp. 12–13: (steps) Tudor Photography; p. 13: (main) Tudor Photography; pp. 14–15: (steps) Tudor Photography; p. 15: (main) Tudor Photography; pp. 16: (main) Tudor Photography; pp. 16–17: (steps) Tudor Photography; pp. 18–19: (steps) Tudor Photography; p. 19: (main) Tudor Photography; pp. 20–21: (steps) Tudor Photography; pp. 21: (main) Jeanette Ryall; pp. 22–23: (steps) Tudor Photography; pp. 23: (main left) Jeanette Ryall, (main right) Tudor Photography; pp. 24–25: (steps) Tudor Photography; p. 25: (main) Tudor Photography; p. 26: (main) Tudor Photography; pp. 26–27: (steps) Tudor Photography; pp. 28–29: (steps) Tudor Photography; p. 29: (main) Tudor Photography.

Every effort has been made to contact copyright holders of material reproduced in this book. Any omissions will be rectified in subsequent printings if notice is given to the publisher.

All the internet addresses (URLs) given in this book were valid at the time of going to press. However, due to the dynamic nature of the internet, some addresses may have changed, or sites may have changed or ceased to exist since publication. While the author and publisher regret any inconvenience this may cause readers, no responsibility for any such changes can be accepted by either the author or the publisher.

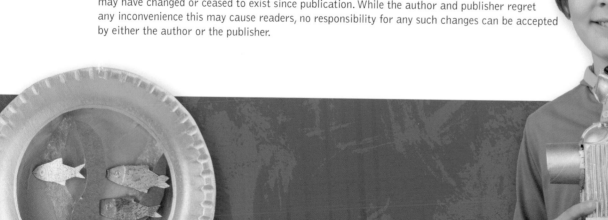

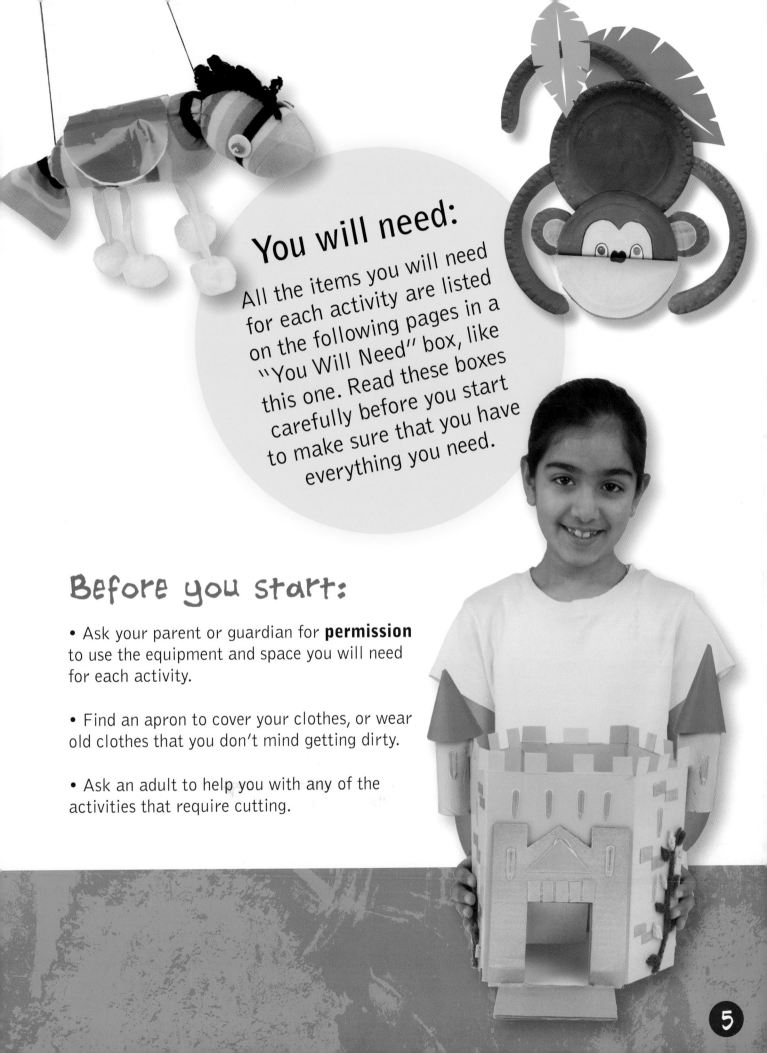

You will need:

All the items you will need for each activity are listed on the following pages in a "You Will Need" box, like this one. Read these boxes carefully before you start to make sure that you have everything you need.

Before you start:

• Ask your parent or guardian for **permission** to use the equipment and space you will need for each activity.

• Find an apron to cover your clothes, or wear old clothes that you don't mind getting dirty.

• Ask an adult to help you with any of the activities that require cutting.

Beautiful buttonfly

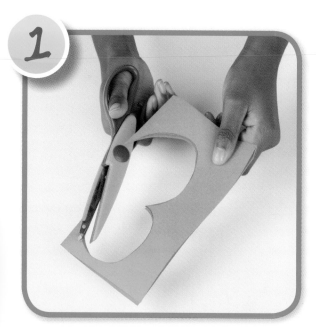

1

You will need:

- pink card
- two **pipe cleaners**
- colourful buttons
- scissors • glue
- glitter glue • pencil

Fold a piece of pink card in half. Then draw the shape of a butterfly wing onto the paper. Cut out the shape.

2

Top Tip

To make different butterflies, change the colour of the card you use.

Open up your butterfly shape. Glue lots of coloured buttons onto the wings. Make sure that you leave a space in the middle of the **design** big enough for the pipe cleaners.

3

Twist together two pipe cleaners, so that the two colours make a striped pattern. Do not twist the ends – these will be **antennae**.

4

Glue the pipe cleaners to the middle of the card shape. Curl the ends of the pipe cleaners to form antennae. Then cover the wings with glitter glue for extra sparkle.

Top Tip
Attach a length of wire to your butterfly to make it stand upright.

Mirror, mirror

You will need:

- cardboard • glue
- colourful ceramic tiles
- shells • pencil
- art knife • mirror
- metal ruler
- small sponge

Use a pencil to draw the size of your mirror frame onto some cardboard. Ask an adult to cut out the frame using an art knife and ruler.

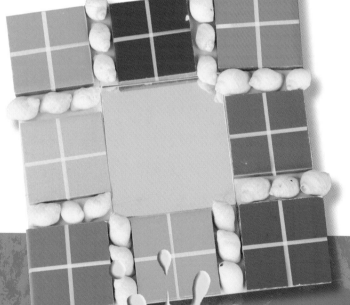

Top Tip
Create a different design by using smaller tiles.

Cover the frame with glue. Create your design by gluing one tile with a row of three shells below the tile to the frame.

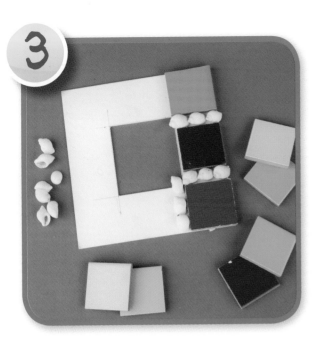

3

Repeat step 2 so that you place one tile and three shells onto each section of the frame. Use a different coloured tile each time.

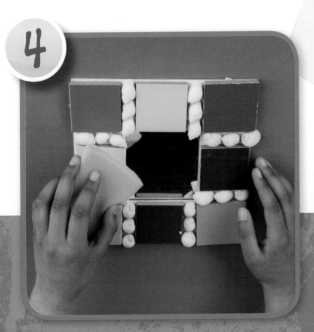

4

When you have completed your design, clean off any **excess** glue with a damp sponge. When dry, glue your mirror to the back of the frame.

Warning
Ask an adult for help when working with glass or mirrors, tiles and knives.

Foil fish

You will need:

- green card
- aluminium foil • pencil
- bubble wrap
- two paper plates
- glue • silver paint
- blue **tissue paper**
- coloured pens
- scissors

Glue some foil onto a sheet of card. Use a pencil to draw a fish shape. Press firmly onto the foil paper. Add **detail,** including the fins, eye and scales of the fish.

Repeat step 1 to create three more fish, remembering to add scales, eyes and fins. Cut out the fish and colour them using coloured pens. Leave them to dry.

Now you can make the **porthole** frame for your fish scene. Take the paper plates and cut out the **base** of one. Glue blue tissue paper onto the base of the other plate.

4

Build your underwater scene by cutting strips of bubble wrap and green card to make seaweed. Glue the bubble wrap strips to the blue tissue base.

5

Glue the green card strips onto the bubble wrap strips to create a 3D effect. Glue your fish between the strips of seaweed so that they appear to swim through them. Leave to dry. Paint the second plate with silver paint and add some glue to the inside edge. Seal the edges of the plates together.

Top Tip

Why not add a treasure chest to your scene?

Spoon puppet

You will need:

- wooden spoon • paintbrush
- white, red, pink and black paint
- black fabric (15 cm square)
- stuffing • scissors
- black wool • star stickers
- glue • card
- gold and purple fabric
- sticky tape • rubber band

1

Paint your spoon pink and leave it to dry. Then paint on white circles for the eyes, red **nostrils**, a red mouth and the black eyebrows, moustache and beard.

2

Roll up a large ball of stuffing and fix it onto the top of the spoon handle with some sticky tape.

3

Wrap the black fabric around the spoon handle. Then **secure** it into position with a rubber band. Cut a length of gold fabric and a length of purple fabric.

4

Add some star stickers to the hat and the fabric of your puppet to complete it.

Top Tip
You can make other puppets. Try making a witch in a red dress!

Wrap the gold and purple fabric around the neck of your puppet. To make a hat, cut a triangle from the black fabric and glue it onto some card. Cut some lengths of black wool and glue them to the back of the hat. Then glue your hat to your puppet.

Junk van

You will need:

- empty plastic cupcake tray
- cardboard square • small pie tin
- sticky tape • glue • foam ring
- purple, red and yellow card • scissors
- empty sweets tube
- foil • **corrugated card**

Cut out these shapes from the coloured card, corrugated card and cardboard square. Arrange them as shown above.

Glue down the small pie tin and cupcake cup tray for wheels. Glue the foam ring onto the pie tin.

Top Tip
Use foil to make headlights for your van.

3

Cover your empty tube in foil and tape it into position. Cut a strip of red card about 2.5 cm wide and tape it onto the end of the tube. Glue the tube to the top of your van.

4

Cut out lightning bolts and glue them onto the door. Then cut out yellow flames and glue them onto the bonnet. Cut out some flames, wrap them in foil and stick them onto the **exhaust**.

15

Egg box robot

You will need:

- two egg boxes • scissors
- two cardboard tubes • silver paint • paintbrush • glue
- large and small buttons
- empty yoghurt pot
- corrugated cardboard
- sticky tape

1

To make the body of the robot, cut two egg boxes in half. Do not throw away any parts of the boxes as you will need them later.

2

Glue the two egg box lids together and leave them to dry. From the base of one egg box, cut out two egg containers and put them to one side. These will be your robot's eyes.

3

Fold back the cut edge. This will help the tube to stick to the body.

Cut the cardboard tube in half. Then cut lots of small slits about 1 cm in length along one end of each section of the two tubes.

4

Tape the cut edges of the two tubes to the robot. Cut two slits in the round part of the "eyes" and glue the eyes onto the top tube section.

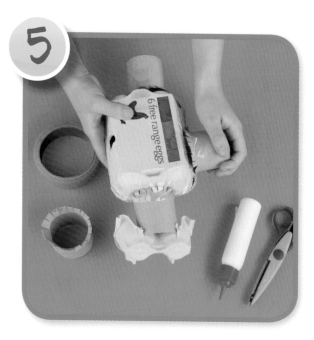

5 Repeat step 3 to cut two more cardboard tubes to make the robot's arms. Glue them onto the sides of the body.

7 Paint your robot with silver paint and leave it to dry. You may need to apply a few **coats** of paint. Once dry, glue on some buttons for the eyes.

6 Stick a piece of corrugated cardboard to the robot's body. Glue the yoghurt pot to the bottom tube for the robot's feet.

8 Glue some gold and red buttons to the front of the robot's body to decorate it. Your egg box robot is now complete!

Top tip
You can use gold paint to make another robot character.

Hanging monkey

You will need:

- four paper plates
- light brown, dark brown and red paint • paintbrush
- scissors • glue
- black pen

Collect three of the paper plates. Cut off the edges of two of the plates. Fold one of the plates in half to make the monkey's mouth.

Paint the inside of the monkey's mouth red and the outside with a light brown colour. Paint the third, uncut plate a dark brown colour.

Now paint the second cut plate. Paint the monkey's head, eyes and nose on the top half of the plate. Once dry, add detail with a black pen to the eyes and nose.

Top tip
Paint "Do not **disturb**" or "Up to monkey business" to make a door plate!

4

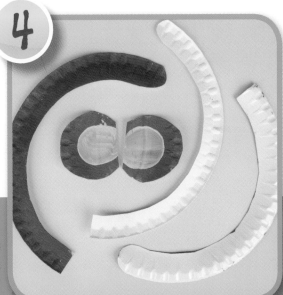

Use the trimmed edges you cut from the plates to create the monkey's arms and tail. Paint them brown. Cut two ear shapes from another paper plate and paint as shown above.

5

Glue the mouth of the monkey to the face. Then glue the head to the body and glue on the arms and tail. Finally, glue the ears onto your monkey to complete it.

In the frame

1

Draw the shape and size of your picture frame onto a sheet of thick card. Carefully cut out the centre hole.

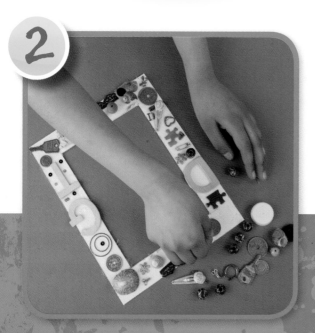

2

Decorate your frame with shells, old jigsaw pieces, buttons, coins and any other junk you like. Glue the junk onto the frame.

3

When you have completed gluing the junk onto the frame, leave it to dry to make sure it is securely fixed to the frame.

4

Cut a piece of paper to fit the back of your frame. Glue a photograph onto the paper and glue it to the back of your frame.

Complete your picture frame by gluing coloured pipe cleaners to the inside edges of your frame. Glue more pipe cleaners to the outside edges.

Top tip

Frame a favourite photograph with your picture frame.

Super rocket

You will need:

- plastic bottle • colourful pen lids
- two plastic cups • two foil cups
- two colourful bottle tops
- one cardboard tube • sticky tape
- three juice cartons
- colourful paper • foil
- scissors • glue
- drinks can pull

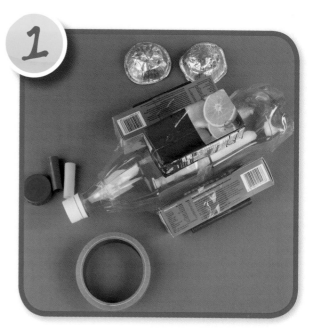

1

Use sticky tape to attach the three juice cartons to each of the three sides of the bottle.

Attach the foil cups to the base of the rocket, then attach the small plastic cups to the foil cups.

Top tip
Cut a slit in your circle to help make the cone shape.

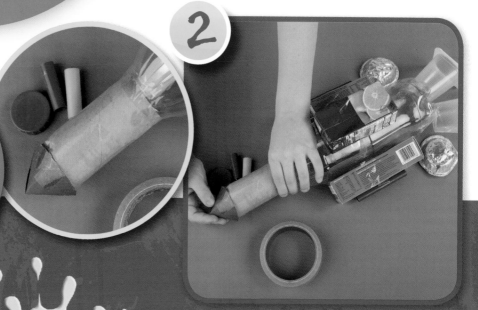

2

Cut a circle from your colourful paper and fold it into a cone shape. Tape the edges and attach the cone to the cardboard tube. Use sticky tape to attach the cardboard tube to the rocket, as shown.

3

Cover your **entire** rocket shape with foil. Don't worry if the foil tears, just cover it with another piece and tape into position.

4

Cut three strips of colourful paper and glue them around the rocket. You can shape some of the strips into your favourite number! Use sticky tape to attach the bottle tops and pen lids to the rocket.

For windows, tape colourful paper circles to the inside of the drinks can pull and stick it onto the rocket!

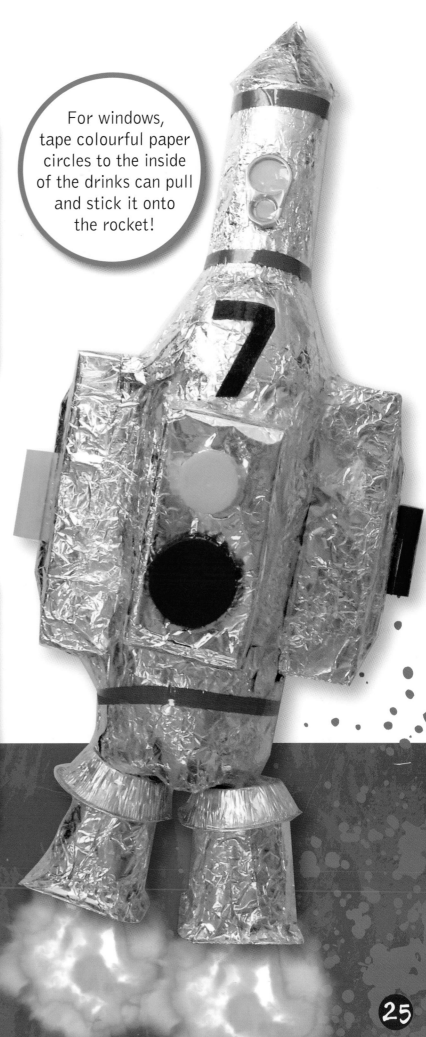

Horse puppet

You will need:

- one striped sock • buttons
- packing tape • needle and black thread • scissors • black wool • ribbon • stuffing
- sticky tape • pompoms
- sheet of paper • glue

1 Fill one end of your sock with some stuffing. Tie the end of the sock with thread to hold the stuffing in position. This will be the head of your horse puppet.

2 Fill the middle of the sock with more stuffing to make the body of the horse. Tie the end with thread to make the shape of the body. The end of the sock will form the horse puppet's tail.

For the puppet strings, attach a length of thread to the front and back of the horse.

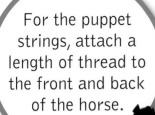

Top tip

Use the strings to make your horse dance!

Stick some strips of brown packing tape onto a sheet of paper. Cut out a circle and tape it onto the horse's back for a saddle.

3

Sew a yellow button onto one side of the head. Glue a smaller blue button on top to make an eye. Repeat on the other side of the head to make the second eye. For the mane, cut pieces of black wool and sew onto the head.

4

For the front legs, cut two pieces of ribbon 15 cm long. Sew a pompom to each end of the ribbon. Sew the middle of each ribbon to the horse's tummy. Repeat to make the back legs.

27

Fairy-tale castle

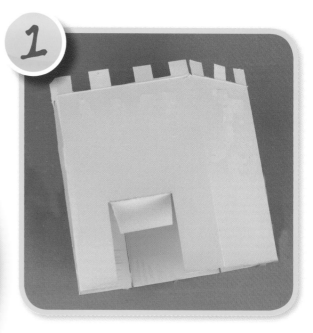

Open up your cereal box and flatten the sides. On the inside of the box, draw the shape of a castle. Cut a door into the front of the box and paint it blue.

For the windows, cut off the end of the drinks stirrers. Glue them onto your castle walls. Cut some brick shapes from the white card and glue them onto the walls. Paint the bricks and windows silver.

Cut a cardboard tube into two pieces and paint them blue. Cut two triangles from red card and roll into cones. Tape the edges together. Place the cones on top of the tubes. Add some curved drinks stirrer pieces for windows.

4

Glue your finished **turrets** to the sides of the castle. To make **vines**, cut and glue a piece of dark green sponge to the castle walls. Cut some leaves from a lighter green sponge.

5

Make the **drawbridge** by cutting a cardboard square. Then cut the shape of the castle entrance from cardboard and cover it with gold paint. Glue it to the front of the castle. Position the drawbridge in front of the entrance.

Glossary

antennae feelers of an insect

assortment lots of different types of one thing

base bottom of something

coats coverings or layers

corrugated card card with a bumpy surface

design pattern or different shapes that make an image

detail fine lines or features

disturb unexpectedly interupt someone

drawbridge bridge-like door on a castle that can be raised or lowered to let people in or out

entire all of something

excess leftover material that is not needed

exhaust rear pipe of a vehicle through which fumes are given off

nostrils openings on the nose or face through which air is breathed

permission allowed to do something

pipe cleaners lengths of thin wire covered in a soft material

porthole small, round window of a boat or ship

secure safe, or firmly fixed

tissue paper very thin, soft paper

turrets rounded towers of a castle

vines plants that can grow on walls of buildings

Find out more

Books

Bit by Bit: Projects for Your Odds and Ends (Creative Crafts), Mari Bolte (Raintree, 2017)

Busting Boredom with Art Projects (Boredom Busters), Mary Boone (Raintree, 2018)

Lazy Crafternoon, Stella Fields (Raintree, 2017)

Website

www.bbc.co.uk/cbbc/games/cbbc-picture-maker
Create your own digital pictures using paints, stickers, glitter and more.

Index

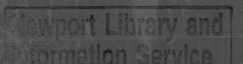